THE GHOSTLY TALES OF NEW MEXICO

Published by Arcadia Children's Books
A Division of Arcadia Publishing
Charleston, SC
www.arcadiapublishing.com

Copyright © 2022 by Arcadia Children's Books
All rights reserved

Spooky America is a trademark of Arcadia Publishing, Inc.

First published 2022

ISBN 9781540252241
Library of Congress Control Number: 2022932229

All images used courtesy of Shutterstock.com; p. 40 Gimas/Shutterstock.com; p.52 rawf8/Shutterstock.com; p. 86 William Silver/Shutterstock.com.

Notice: The information in this book is true and complete to the best of our knowledge. It is offered without guarantee on the part of the author or Arcadia Publishing. The author and Arcadia Publishing disclaim all liability in connection with the use of this book.

All rights reserved. No part of this book may be reproduced or transmitted in any form whatsoever without prior written permission from the publisher except in the case of brief quotations embodied in critical articles and reviews.

Spooky America

THE GHOSTLY TALES OF NEW MEXICO

SHELLI TIMMONS

Adapted from *Haunted Hotels and Ghostly Getaways of New Mexico* by Donna Blake Birchell

New Mexico

Colorado

Arizona

Texas

Table of Contents & Map Key

Introduction 3

1. Chapter 1. Unearthly Albuquerque 7
2. Chapter 2. Creepy Carlsbad 21
3. Chapter 3. Eerie Eagle Nest 33
4. Chapter 4. Ghostly Taos 41
5. Chapter 5. Spooky Santa Fe 53
6. Chapter 6. Supernatural Cimarron 63
7. Chapter 7. Legends of Las Vegas 77
8. Chapter 8. Spirits of Lincoln 87
9. Chapter 9. Chilling Chama 95
10. Chapter 10. Haunted Hatch and Rodey 101

Conclusion 107

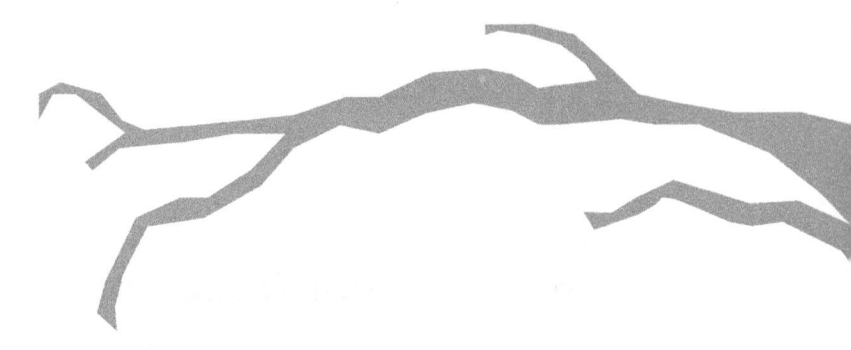

Introduction

New Mexico is the forty-seventh of our fifty American states. Many people still confuse it with the country of Mexico, but it has been a part of the United States of America since 1912. It's known as the Land of Enchantment due to all the spirits roaming around. Okay, maybe it's called that because of its magnificent sunrises and sunsets, bright blue skies, snow-capped mountains, fascinating caves, blooming deserts, vast rolling plains, and expansive lakes and rivers. With so many beautiful places to haunt, no wonder the ghosts don't want to leave.

Native American culture is important here. Members of over twenty nations live in New Mexico. Their influences can be found in art, architecture, and traditions dating back to long before New Mexico was a state and continuing today.

Spanish settlers came and introduced their own culture, much of which is also still evident today. The Spanish influence is seen throughout the state in the form of mission churches, chapels, and cathedrals.

Settlers continued to come, and each new group contributed new cultural influences, including food, music, art, and religion. They also brought their own beliefs about the spirit world. New Mexico is widely regarded

Introduction

as a highly spiritual place for many different reasons, not just because of ghosts. But make no mistake, there are plenty of ghosts who claim the Land of Enchantment as their eternal home.

Disembodied spirits linger all across New Mexico. Hotels seem to be particularly good places to meet one. Would you like to encounter a ghost on your next vacation? If so, this is the book for you!

In the pages that follow, you will learn about some of New Mexico's most famous towns and their ghostly getaways and haunted hotels—along with the spirits who inhabit them, of course. Are you ready?

Let's get to know some new places. And some old ghosts!

Unearthly Albuquerque

The ancient Tewa people long lived on the banks of the Rio Grande. They were here when the Spanish conquistadors (conquerors), led by Francisco Vásquez de Coronado, arrived in search of gold and other riches. This began more than a century of fighting between the local Pueblo people and the Spanish. The Spanish, and later the Americans, took control, and the town of Albuquerque eventually grew due to the railroad, which brought many new residents to the area. Today, Albuquerque is the largest city in New Mexico. The area known as Old Town still thrives, and the city maintains its history and its historical buildings that sit around the central plaza.

The beautiful city of Albuquerque is a celebrated stop on the famous Route 66. Tourists used to travel this road all the way from Illinois to California. Hotels along the way used neon signs to alert weary travelers of available rooms. Many of those

well-known hotels still exist along Route 66 in Albuquerque, but the road is now called Central Avenue. With so much to do in this town, you might be exhausted at the end of the day. It would probably feel pretty good to rest your tired bones in a vintage hotel room after a long, fun-filled day.

But beware! Your night may be long, too, if you get a ghost for a roommate. Especially if you stay at the Painted Lady Bed & Brew.

Walking along Bellamah Avenue, you can't miss the Painted Lady Bed & Brew. It takes up nearly half a city block and is surrounded by lights. Not to mention it has a train car in the yard! It has served many purposes since it was built in 1881, from a grocery store to a saloon. It also provided lodging for travelers in the past. Rumor has it that New Mexico's famous outlaw, Billy the Kid, and Pat Garrett, the man who would eventually take him down, stayed there, too.

Some say the site of the Painted Lady was once Native American land and was part of the Battle of Albuquerque. People may have been buried on or nearby the property.

Back when the Painted Lady was a saloon, the owners did not trust banks. Instead of putting their money in a bank account, they would bury it in coffee cans on the property. Some of the money has been found, but it's hard to say if they got it all. There may be some spirits hanging around who know exactly

where to dig for the rest of it, but they haven't told anyone yet. Even a ghost doesn't want to give up the location of buried treasure!

No matter what the spirits of the Painted Lady share or keep to themselves, the owner says they are a bonus to the all-around atmosphere of the place. The owner's suite is said to be the most haunted room of the house. Its ghosts are sometimes funny but other times terrifying. Many former owners would not enter the space.

Legend says a husband found his wife with another man there once. He murdered them both with an axe. The man who was killed was apparently in no hurry to leave. He hung around to haunt the place. Women seem to find his room disturbing more often than men.

The current owner experienced so many strange problems during the renovations that he called in a medium to perform a spiritual cleanse. The medium reported that there were three ghosts in permanent residence. The scariest one liked the corner and did not want to leave. The owner tried to make a deal with the spirit: "you leave me alone and I'll leave you alone." He soon found out the spirit wasn't going to live up to his side of the bargain.

This bothersome ghost began to torment the owner's three-legged dog, whose name was Bill Murray (Murray for short). Murray would yelp in pain, and he had bloody marks from being bitten by something unseen.

Two local psychic mediums were called in to set up a demon trap. This stubborn spirit shared the dog's first name of Bill. Demon Bill was described by the mediums as being in his forties and nicely dressed in the style of the late 1880s. He did not leave quietly, but he was eventually banished. Murray was very happy to see him go.

When the owner's mother helped him decorate to welcome guests for the International Balloon Fiesta, a very strange thing happened. As she was removing plastic from the new refrigerator, she turned to her son and asked him what he'd just said. "I haven't said anything," he told her. His mother laughed and told him that was strange because she had heard a man ask, "Can you grab me a beer?"

Murray the dog has reacted to another nonhuman spirit as well. A medium says this one is the spirit of another dog. The ghost dog upsets Murray when it messes with his food bowl. It's hard to blame Murray for getting upset about that. No one wants their food messed with, especially not by a ghost!

A family member of the original builders says the three ghosts who reside at the property are all nice. The owner was told he could expect to hear a "shuffle, shuffle, cane, jiggle" at around 12:30 a.m. each morning. This sound is apparently made by a former resident

named Uncle Charlie doing a nightly check of the doors to keep the guests safe. Well, there are certainly worse things a ghost could do. If you have to have a spirit roaming around, Uncle Charlie sounds like a pretty good option.

But the Painted Lady is not the only haunted hotel in the Albuquerque area. You might encounter spirits at the Red Horse Vineyard Bed and Breakfast in the South Valley.

Guests of the Red Horse have called it an "oasis in the desert." It was built by the Ellis family, who came from Europe in 1870. Later, they planted grapes they had brought from the old country and added a vineyard and a winery. The Londene family bought the property in 1968.

The remains of the original house collapsed in 1972, but the Londenes salvaged and restored as much as possible. Even a game room that was added much later makes use of windows from the original collapsed house.

The Red Horse is named for the red Dalecarlian horse, a type of wooden carved horse that was originally used as a children's toy. These painted horses originated in Dalarna, Sweden. Carl Londene and his daughter are both artists, and they produce a ceramic version of this horse to honor their Swedish heritage. Prior to her death in 2013,

Carl Londene's wife, Donna, was very sensitive to the presence of spirits in the house. She would carry on conversations with beings no one else was able to see. This was normal for Donna. Interacting with the ghosts didn't bother her at all.

Two little girls in blue were some of Donna's favorite visitors. The girls would skip up and down the upstairs hallway, giggling

and playing. Recent visitors have asked about the children playing in the hallway, even when there were no children staying on the property at the time.

If you see two little girls running in the hallway at the Red Horse and you tell them to stop, they might not hear you. In fact, they might not even be alive.

Another frequent spirit who visited Donna was a man dressed in Victorian clothing. He would appear at the foot of her bed, and the two would carry on long conversations. Remember, if you stay in this lovely bed-and-breakfast and a ghostly man appears at the foot of your bed, don't freak out. Maybe he just wants to talk. Maybe. But then again, no one can make any guarantees when it comes to ghosts.

Creepy Carlsbad

Carlsbad was founded in 1888 by Charles Bishop Eddy, who had moved to the area from New York. He named the settlement after himself: Eddy. It was Charles Eddy's dream to have a perfect society free of any vice (immoral behavior or bad habits), especially alcohol. But convincing people to come from around the world to settle on a flat piece of land in the middle of a desert wouldn't be easy. The saving grace for the region was the Pecos River.

Local cowboys called the area Rattlesnake Flats due to the extremely large population of rattlesnakes. Running cattle through the area was dangerous, not only because of the venomous snakes but also because of snake holes. Stepping into one of those holes could turn the ankle of a steer or a horse in an instant. Contests to round up and get rid of the snakes became popular.

Despite all the snakes and the flat land, investors and settlers alike were unable to resist Charles Eddy's charm. The town grew by leaps and bounds to become the county seat. It became home to emigrants from Italy, Switzerland, and Germany. The town was

an agricultural success thanks to one of the largest irrigation projects in the United States. Charles Eddy found an excellent way to make use of the Pecos River.

He worked with three partners to turn the arid desert landscape into thriving farmland. Soon, cotton, grapes, alfalfa, sugar beets, and peaches were growing well in Eddy thanks to the favorable condition of the soil.

In 1890, the railroad came to the area and made getting crops to market much easier. The town was now truly connected to the rest of the country. Charles Eddy left to start new ventures elsewhere, and the town was renamed Carlsbad.

It is a popular place to visit today due to Carlsbad Caverns National Park, the Living Desert Zoo, and Gardens State Park. Known as "Cave City," this once sleepy small town is now bustling with activity and has a bright future. And ghosts, of course.

You'll find them at the Trinity Hotel, built in 1892. The Trinity was also once the home of the town's founder, Charles Eddy, as well as Sheriff Pat Garrett. It was neglected over the years and sadly ended up on New Mexico's Endangered Historic Buildings list. But now it has been restored into a beautiful hotel. Who would ever want to check out?

Miss Ruby has been making her presence known at the Trinity since the hotel opened in 2008. She usually hangs out in her favorite spot on the second floor of the restaurant in a secret room. Insider tip: if you ask, your server will probably show you the entrance to this hidden room.

Ruby is said to patiently watch over the staff as they prepare tables for the day's customers. She likes to call the staff by name. What a thoughtful ghost! But she must have strong opinions about music, because she has been known to turn off the sound system when she doesn't like the song.

It is believed Ruby was the secretary of the Carlsbad Irrigation District around 1888. Room 206 is her favorite to haunt. This room contains the vintage safe, and it was originally her office. Rooms 201, 206, and 207 were one big office during her time. Ruby is protective of what was once her workspace.

She is also a prankster who is very creative with her pranks. One guest reported that he and his family were unable to find the towels from their bathroom one morning. They finally located them on top of the window ledge—about nineteen feet off the floor! A ladder had to be used to get the towels down for the family. Ha! Good one, Ruby.

Ghost hunters who investigate the property have told the owners about another spirit who resides there. This entity is allegedly a caretaker who worked at the Trinity building for forty years. The staff and owners call him "the Glass Breaker" because he likes to break glassware to express his disapproval. Nothing like a little flying glass to keep the workday interesting, especially when it's thrown by a ghost. Yikes!

The hotel's vineyards, located twelve miles north at Seven Rivers, also hold some spooky stories. This is the reason for the vineyard's wine label, The Spirits of Seven Rivers. To accommodate the construction of Brantley Dam, the Seven Rivers Cemetery had to be moved. When you're moving the remains of the dead, there is always a chance a spirt might show up as a result. To be fair, they were probably just peacefully minding their afterlife business when they got disturbed. Why wouldn't they rise up and check out the disruption?

On occasion, a cowboy on horseback will ride through the wall of the grape processing

building. No big deal, just a cowboy and a horse coming through the wall. Yeah, not your average day in most places. But then again, not every place is built on what was once a cemetery.

A little girl, who is clearly not among the living, has been seen playing in the grapevines. Both she and the cowboy match the descriptions of people buried in relocated graves.

During the 1880s, Seven Rivers was known as the most violent town in New Mexico. It was reported in the local newspaper that you could read the paper by the light of gunfire at night. When the graves were opened, the town's violent past became evident. Not too many citizens died of natural causes.

Some authorities claim the mile-long stretch of road that runs through Seven Rivers

is one of the most haunted stretches of highway in the state. The New Mexico State Police have records of people going off the road to avoid a woman in a white dress crossing the highway. She and other apparitions seem to appear out of nowhere. They disappear just as quickly, but you can be sure they'll be back—when you least expect them. Watch out for ghosts in the road!

Eerie Eagle Nest

The land now known as Eagle Nest was once home to the Ute and Jicarilla Apache tribes. Founded by T.D. Neal as Therma in 1919, it took the name Eagle Nest when the official post office was established in 1935.

Cutting and selling ice blocks from the lake became one of the largest industries. Men were hired to travel out on the ice and cut chunks, which were then stored in sawdust in icehouses. Many families made their living doing this in the winter months. Eagle Nest became a good rest stop for travelers who had just ascended the steep Cimarron Canyon. Gambling was a huge draw, and many visitors came to play at the roulette wheels, gaming tables, and slot machines scattered throughout the town until raids in the 1940s put an end to all that. When the gambling halls heard of an upcoming raid, they would lower all their slot machines and other equipment into the lake to hide it from police officers, who would destroy them if they found them.

There are probably some interesting things at the bottom of that lake. If only the ghosts around it could write it all down or tell someone. . . . On second thought, they might have more interesting tales to tell about things that went on above the water. And given the town's violent past, some of those tales might be best told with the lights on.

Take the story of the hauntings at the Laguna Vista Lodge, for example. It was built in 1897 as a gambling hall, saloon, and restaurant called El Monte. It was allegedly constructed of stolen railroad ties from Elizabethtown, five

miles away, which is now a ghost town. Some of these ties are still visible in rooms today.

In the early 1900s, the El Monte made so much money from gambling that the owners would often arm themselves while taking the profits from the saloon to their living quarters. They were afraid they would be robbed in that short distance. During the 1920s and 1930s, it was at its busiest point. It was during this time that the name was changed to Laguna Vista Lodge.

New owners took over in the early 1950s. The Laguna Vista Lodge has been a temporary home to many actors during the filming of movies or TV shows in the area. The hotel has also been featured in several magazines. The ghosts at Laguna Vista Lodge are celebrities themselves, at least to the people who run the hotel.

The main spirit present at Laguna Vista Lodge is named Eleanor. She was a newlywed who stayed there with her husband for their honeymoon. One day he went out hunting and never returned. Eleanor was left stranded at the lodge with no money or job. She had nowhere to go, so she began working at the hotel.

Sadly, it is believed Eleanor died of a broken heart. An elegant white dress, which could have been hers, is framed with dried roses and stands in her room as a gentle reminder of her days as a young bride.

Eleanor's ghost remains at the old Laguna Vista Lodge, possibly still waiting for her husband to return. Staff say she is harmless. She has been known to haunt the dining room and sometimes startles the bartender by calling her name. Some claim Eleanor likes it to be nice and quiet in the hotel. She has been known to turn off radios and has even cautioned children not to make so much noise. Unnamed spirits haunt the lodge as well. Guests have reported trays and glasses moving on their own. Vacuum cleaners sometimes turn on by themselves. Some ghosts make messes, but it sounds like these want to help clean instead.

Frequently, the spirit of a small boy named David is seen in the kitchen. He is unhappy and is said to be constantly crying. The owner of Laguna Vista Lodge has been told that at least 22 different spirits haunt the property. That's a lot of ghostly guests! One is musical and will play the piano while sitting on a dining room chair. Another prefers to throw rolling pins in the kitchen. Radios without batteries turn on by themselves. Poor Eleanor probably stays far away from those noise-makers.

Investigators say the ghosts at Laguna Vista Lodge are harmless, though you might want to watch out for flying rolling pins in the kitchen.

CHAPTER 4

Ghostly Taos

Taos dates back to 1540, when explorer Captain Hernando Alvarado arrived with the Coronado Expedition in search of the legendary Seven Cities of Gold. The explorers believed they had found the gold they sought, because the surface of the Taos Pueblo glistened in the sunlight as if it were covered in flecks of gold.

It was not real gold. The earth used to make

the pueblo had a high content of the mineral mica, which sparkles and can look like gold. Spanish settlers moved to the area and set up homes near the pueblo for protection. The explorers were only fooled by the mica for a short time, but settlers remained in the village. By 1760, it was known as Don Fernando de Taos by the Spanish inhabitants. The name was eventually shortened to Taos, which means "red willow" in the native Tewa language.

Taos continued to grow and became one of the first artist colonies established in the United States.

Along with the artistic vibe and great hiking opportunities, Taos also offers whitewater rafting, skiing, and snowboarding. But

many come to see the Taos Pueblo, the best preserved, still-inhabited example of Puebloan culture, dating to 1325.

Taos has also come to be known for strange phenomena in the area. Some say a low-frequency hum can be heard just outside Taos city limits. The source behind the hum has never been found. It is also reported that the entire valley has a magnetic quality—a vortex—that draws many to the region. Could it be this strange energy that attracts ghosts?

You'll find them at the Hacienda del Sol ("House of the Sun" in English). Built in 1804, it was a private residence where many famous authors and artists have also been among the honored guests throughout the years.

Today, it's a hotel that's popular for weddings and celebrations of all sorts. A cozy fireplace in the dining room chases away the chill of northern New Mexico mornings and evenings. But it doesn't ward off the ghosts who haunt the hacienda.

The presence of Mabel Dodge Luhan is felt in the main part of the house, especially in her private room behind an arched, powder-blue door. Mabel was a well-known socialite, and her space is still decorated with original artwork given to her by her famous artist friends.

Another spirit detected at the hacienda is Mabel's fourth husband, Tony, who was a native of the Taos Pueblo. Both Mabel and Tony were said to be larger than life on earth. It seems they are still very much attached to their earthly home.

A faint sound of drums can sometimes be heard coming from Mabel's room. Tony was rarely seen without his drums, and many believe this is him playing them privately beyond the blue door for his wife. And they may not want to be disturbed. Guests sometimes report that when they insert their key into the door of this room, it is gently pushed back out from the other side.

One guest reported having a lengthy conversation with a man sitting at the fireplace in the dining room. During their conversation, the man asked her to take down certain Native American artifacts hanging in the room at the time. When she was shown a photograph of Tony Luhan, the guest confirmed he was indeed the man who made the request.

But the Hacienda del Sol isn't the only haunted hotel in Taos. The Historic Taos Inn was the former home and office of Dr. Thomas P. Martin and his wife, Helen. The hotel started out in the 1800s as a combination of several adobe houses encircling a plaza. That plaza is the hotel lobby today. Covering the fountain in the main lobby is an impressive two-and-a-half story cupola topped with stained glass. The fountain was once the community well.

Dr. Martin was the only physician in the county. He moved to Taos in 1890 and purchased the largest home on the plaza. Today, this structure is the Doc Martin Restaurant. The kitchen was his surgical area, and the first dining area to the left functioned as a birthing room.

Several spirits haunt the Historic Taos Inn. One of the most famous is the ghost of Arthur Manby, who was murdered in a small building on the property. Manby was known as the most hated man in Taos due to his scheming ways. He committed all sorts of frauds to trick people into giving him money. He may have even committed a murder of his own.

Manby was murdered (or not?) on July 1, 1929, by decapitation. By the time he was found in his home, his head was in such bad shape that it was impossible to positively identify him. Some people believed it wasn't him at all. They thought Manby may have murdered someone else in his home so he could escape to Europe and avoid being punished for his crimes. Nothing was ever proven.

Manby's room, number 109, is now part of the Historic Taos Inn. The figure of a man who fits Manby's description has been seen standing by the fireplace. The housekeeping staff often feels cold temperatures in the room.

The Doc Martin Restaurant kitchen, which shares a common wall with Arthur Manby's former home, has unusual activity from time to time as well. Pots and pans and small appliances fly off the counters on their own. Doors open and close without any human help, and lights commonly flash in the dining room.

Rumor has it that a cowboy wearing jangling spurs wanders the halls of the main lobby area. He has also been known to visit certain rooms just to say hello.

Room 102 has an unexplained faint smell of roses. The figure of a tall woman sometimes appears in the doorway of Room 106. It is said she exits the room through a mirror that is left crooked after her departure. Room 206 used to have figures painted on the fireplace. After several guests refused to stay there and left suddenly, the fireplace was repainted. The problems in Room 206 stopped after the figures were painted over.

The Adobe Bar has a regular apparition who likes to call out the names of staff members when they are all alone after closing.

If you're in search of lots of spirit activity, it seems like the Historic Taos Inn has plenty of opportunities for ghost spotting. You'll probably be safe there as long as you stay out of the kitchen. And maybe don't stay in Room 109 unless you want to deal with the

ghost of the most hated man in Taos. On the other hand, maybe you can solve the mystery and find out once and for all who was really murdered there. That swindling ghost is the only one who knows for sure. But are you brave enough to ask him?

Spooky Santa Fe

Santa Fe ("holy faith") is the oldest capital city in the United States. It's called the "City Different" and it lives up to its nickname.

Santa Fe has become popular among celebrities, and the non-famous as well, as a place to take a break from the stress of their daily lives. Many of the shops surrounding the Santa Fe Plaza are original structures from the

1600s. With so much history, it's not surprising that Santa Fe has its share of ghost stories.

La Posada de Santa Fe Resort and Spa is one of the most renowned resorts in Santa Fe.

It was built in 1882 by wealthy Santa Fe merchant, Abraham Staab, and his wife, Julia. In the 1990s, it was restored into the luxury resort you find today.

Julia Staab loved her grand home and was happy there until a tragedy changed her personality. Her spirit remains and is said to be a gentle ghost. She and Abraham both grew up

in Germany. Abraham came to Santa Fe at the age of fifteen to work with his brother in Santa Fe. The brothers opened a dry goods store on the Santa Fe Plaza in 1859. By 1865, Abraham had made enough money to return to Germany and marry Julia on Christmas Day.

The couple had seven children and lived a happy life until the death of their eighth child, a daughter. Julia grew severely depressed after the loss and was often ill. She frequently went back to Germany for spa treatments.

Julia tried several times to have another child, but sadly it never happened. She eventually secluded herself in her room, where she died in 1896 at the age of fifty-two. Her ghost is most often seen at the top of the staircase that was once the front steps of her mansion, dressed in black. This staircase now leads to the guestrooms upstairs.

She has also been seen sitting quietly on a chair in the bar, weeping. Other accounts report her sending bar glasses and ladies' makeup flying across the room. Julia loved to take baths, and guests who have stayed in her room have reported bath water spontaneously running in the middle of the night. The first known encounter with Julia's ghost happened in 1970 after the furnace broke. When workers tried to enter the furnace room, it was locked. A phone call from Julia's room, which was unoccupied, rang at the front desk. A woman's voice stated, "This is my house. Why isn't the furnace working? I'll get it fixed." The front desk reported that ten minutes later, the furnace did indeed start working. At that point, the door unlocked on its own. Girls (and girl ghosts!) can do anything, including fix their own furnace, apparently.

The spirit of an old Native American man is also present at La Posada de Santa Fe Resort and Spa. He is said to have died in 1096, nearly 800 years before the Staabs' mansion was built on the property.

La Fonda on the Plaza Santa Fe sits on the site of Santa Fe's first inn, which was built in 1607. It was located directly at the start of the Santa Fe Trail and the end of the Camino Real, the main road leading up from Mexico to the area. La Fonda on the Plaza and the inns that came before it provided lodging to the many travelers headed west to the goldfields or east to more civilized surroundings.

As with any hotel sporting a four-hundred-year history, rumors of spirits at La Fonda on the Plaza abound. New Mexico was an unruly territory in the 1800s, and many disagreements were settled at the end of a pistol. Some spirits still find it hard to rest there.

In 1862, a Texas cowboy began to shoot up La Fonda in revenge for a friend. He shot a

lawyer in the stomach and another man in the arm. The cowboy was lynched (hanged without a trial) in the backyard of the hotel. His shadow is reportedly seen hanging from the tree when the light is right on the patio.

At one point, a deep well sat in the center of La Fonda's dining room, now known as La Plazuela. Legend states that a traveling salesman leapt to his death in the well after losing all his company's money in a card game. An apparition of a man who walks to the center of the dining room, jumps, and then disappears has been reported by staff over the years. Nothing was written about this man's death in the local newspapers at the time. The first written report of the event was in 1991.

Room 510, the Honeymoon Suite, is supposedly haunted by a young bride who was murdered there. A different version of the story about her death states she and her husband arrived at the hotel in the 1930s. The husband began drinking heavily in the bar and got into an argument with the bartender, who shot him dead at the bottom of the steps going to up to

the room. The bride found her husband's body and pulled out a gun and shot herself.

No reports can be found of this incident, but if you stay in Room 510, don't be surprised if the ghost of a young bride shows up. Regardless of how she died, it seems certain she never checked out of the hotel.

CHAPTER 6

Supernatural Cimarron

Cimarron means "wild and unruly." That was a perfect choice for the name of this town, once the epitome of a Wild West settlement. But its history goes much deeper. Once home to the Ute, Anasazi, and Jicarilla Apache, Cimarron became the center of the region when gold and silver miners, cowboys, and businessmen all came to the well-named mountain community in search of fortune.

Ranching saved the town from extinction when the railroad passed it by. Logging and coal mining played a huge role in forming the town. The quaint mountain village now caters to curious tourists. The Philmont Boy Scout Camp, the largest campsite in America, sits just out of town on Urraca Mesa, which holds the record as the mountain most often struck by lightning per year in the state.

The mesa is also the subject of Navajo legends. One legend claims the mountain is the gate to hell and the site of a great battle between humans and the dark forces of evil.

The word *urraca* means "magpie." According to legend, if a magpie calls your name, you will die soon.

Due to the high iron and lodestone content of the mesa, compasses do not work correctly in the area. People hiking there have reported hearing strange voices, having odd animals follow them, and getting the sensation they are being watched always.

If you stay in town in a hotel instead, you might expect other strange encounters—namely, the ghosts!

Cimarron is home to one of the most haunted hotels in all New Mexico—the Express St. James. It was built between 1870 and 1880 by French chef Henri (later changed to Henry) Lambert. Lambert, who was a personal chef to Abraham Lincoln, built the St. James on the recommendation of President Ulysses S. Grant.

Henri Lambert left his home in Nantes, France, at the young age of twelve to work

as an apprentice chef in Le Havre, France. Imagine moving away from home at twelve to become a chef!

He later joined the French navy and was assigned to the nation's first submarine. A ship towed the submarine to the United States with Henri on board. Upon arrival, he joined the Union army and became a cook for Ulysses Grant under the service of Abraham Lincoln.

After the Civil War ended, Henri and his wife came to New Mexico and settled in Elizabethtown. He had hopes of finding his fortune in gold. When he found very little gold, he moved on to Cimarron to open his saloon and hotel there.

At least twenty-seven men died in and around the Express St. James Hotel in documented gunfights between 1872 and 1884. You can still count bullet holes in the ceiling of the hotel's saloon. They remain as evidence of a rowdier time in Cimarron, New Mexico, where outlaws roamed the streets, ready to fight.

During renovations on the hotel in 1901, the tin ceiling tiles were removed to reveal at least four hundred more bullet holes. Legend tells of a local rancher who often drank too much and shot his weapon into the air inside the bar. It is believed many of the bullet holes discovered probably came from the rancher's drunken shooting.

Many known outlaws stayed at the Express St. James during the time of the Wild West, including Buffalo Bill Cody and Annie Oakley. Some think Jesse James stayed several times, always in Room 14. Perhaps some of the outlaw guests may have fired a pistol or two indoors as well.

Most of the hotel's thirteen rooms are named for famous past guests, and the hotel still appears much as it did when it was first built. The wood floors, plastered walls, and wood moldings are reminders of a more elegant but dangerous era. There are no elevators in the original St. James. You will have to take the steep, narrow stairs unless you stay in the modern annex, which the staff jokingly calls the "sissy wing." The new annex not only has the convenience of elevators but it is also not haunted, as far as anyone knows.

With many YouTube videos and internet discussions about the ghosts there, the St. James has gotten the attention of national and international organizations that investigate the paranormal.

The second floor is known for the most activity. All but one of the rooms are roped off with red velvet barriers, and the doors remain open unless occupied by guests. This allows visitors to see and photograph the haunted rooms as they tour the hotel.

Room 18, known as T.J.'s Room, is the only one that stays closed—and padlocked! The public is not allowed to enter this room due to the powerful nature of the entity that resides there. The staff describes T.J. as a cranky, angry ghost with a history of being violent.

Thomas James Wright, a regular at the St. James in the 1880s, would spend his nights gambling, smoking cigars, and drinking whiskey. He once won ownership of the St. James in a poker game. Happy with his winnings, he returned to his second-floor room to get some sleep. He was shot from behind in his room. Barely able to make it the short distance from the doorway to the bed, Wright bled to death there. He never saw his killer.

It is said he holds a grudge to this day and does not like anyone in his room. The staff respects his feelings (and their own safety) by announcing their intentions and asking for permission to enter when they dare. On the extremely rare event someone other than an employee is allowed in T.J.'s Room, tokens of appreciation, such as small bottles of whiskey, playing cards, and cigars are left for him.

Hotel guests have taken up the tradition of leaving a shot glass of whiskey on the ledge of the painted window over the door to his room as a tribute to the unfortunate cowboy. Sometimes, the full shot glasses are empty by morning. A strong odor of cigar smoke has

been detected outside his room during the night. Smoking is not allowed in the hotel, but T.J. doesn't seem to care about that rule.

An episode of the television show *Unsolved Mysteries* featured the story of the ex-wife of the current owner of the St. James, who thought she could get rid of the ghosts in her hotel. She stood outside and informed the spirits there that they could leave and to "just go."

According to eyewitnesses, a large orb exited the hotel just long enough to knock her down and then it returned into the hotel. Staff members are convinced it was T.J. letting her know what he thought about her suggestion.

Across the hall from T.J.'s Room is Room 17, which belonged to Mary Elizabeth Lambert, the wife of the hotel's original owner, Henri. Guests in that room often smell a distinct rose-scented perfume unlike anything manufactured today. It is also reported that Mary Elizabeth likes to play with guests' toes by pinching them in the middle of the night. Maybe she's just making sure they're still alive.

Elegant crystal chandeliers in the upstairs hallway have been known to turn themselves back on after they were turned off by staff members. They are left on all the time now. Giggling children have been heard running up and down the halls when there are no children in the hotel at the time.

There is a small ghost of an old man, nicknamed "Little Imp" by the staff, who likes to play tricks on people by moving objects.

The handsome face of a cowboy is known to randomly appear in an upstairs mirror.

The Express St. James Hotel has two large binders in the main lobby containing handwritten accounts from guests of their experiences there. Many of the stories

are similar despite being written several years apart.

If you think an otherworldly encounter would make your vacation memorable in all the best ways, put the Express St. James Hotel on your list. Don't forget to bring a few small gifts for T.J. And if you're in Room 17, sleep with your shoes on to protect your toes from Mary Elizabeth's cold squeezing fingers.

Chapter 7

Legends of Las Vegas

Las Vegas, New Mexico—not to be confused with the famed gambling city in Nevada—is located in a perfect spot for those interested in history. The town plaza was the site where Stephen W. Kearney claimed New Mexico for the United States in 1846 during the Mexican-American War. In the 1870s, Las Vegas was the largest town in New Mexico.

And by the 1880s, it had become one of the most violent.

Like some other Wild West towns in New Mexico, Las Vegas saw plenty of outlaws, including Jesse James and Billy the Kid.

Doc Holliday's first shoot-out took place there. Doc owned a saloon in downtown Las Vegas. He shot an Army scout named Mike Gordon on Centre Street (now Lincoln Avenue) right in front of the saloon. It was after this that Doc Holliday moved on to Dodge City, Kansas.

The town plaza had a windmill frame that served as a "hanging tree." It was a reminder

of the constant violence that took place in the town and a warning to those who might be thinking of causing trouble.

As the location for many movies and television shows, Las Vegas attracts tourists who come to see the settings of their favorite films and shows. Many visit to experience the local hot springs (natural thermal pools). Because it caters to so many visitors, you'll find a number of hotels here, including the Plaza Hotel, built in 1892.

The exterior of the Plaza Hotel still looks exactly as it did when it was the fanciest hotel in town, complete with a saloon, dance hall,

and thirty-seven guestrooms. There is no shortage of spaces to appreciate—for the living and the dead.

One of the hotel's ghosts is rumored to be Byron T. Mills, who owned the Plaza from 1918 until he died in 1947. He did not take good care of the hotel. It needed so many repairs that he considered tearing it down in 1940. Thankfully, he didn't go through with it. Some say because of the way he neglected the beautiful Plaza he still wanders the halls out of guilt.

Mills is reported to haunt Rooms 310 and 316 most often, but his presence has been felt in other rooms as well. He is particularly fond of women with red hair. His actions are subtle, such as turning the lights on and off or sitting on the bed. He may even lie down next to you. If you stay on the third floor and wake up with the sense that you're not alone in the bed, you could be sleeping with a ghost. Sweet dreams!

Another spirit reported at the Plaza Hotel is a small girl who likes the company of women and having her picture taken. She has been photographed many times sitting next to women in the lobby. The women don't even realize the girl is there. This little ghost isn't a troublemaker, she just wants to stay close. And photobomb.

The Plaza isn't the only haunted hotel in Las Vegas. You'll also find ghostly guests at the Crow's Nest Bed & Breakfast, one of the most

notable buildings in Las Vegas. Its three-story octagonal tower makes it easy to spot.

Dr. H.J. Mueller and his wife, Zella, built the home in 1881. Dr. Henry J. Mueller was a jealous man, especially regarding his beautiful wife. It is said that he would not allow her to go outdoors except to pace the widow's walk on the roof.

The current owner of the property, Dolly Crow, reports that Zella is still there, but she is a quiet presence who does not make herself known to many people. She has touched Dolly on the shoulder. A guest from Washington, DC, had a brief encounter with Zella. He reported that Zella asked him if he was okay.

Another spirit at the Crow's Nest is Zella's son, who died

in the house at a young age. He is a playful spirit who loves children. The owner's young nephew became frustrated during a visit whenever he saw the little boy ghost and no one else could. The ghost enjoyed playing with the boy so much that he followed the family home. He is reported to have caused some havoc there until he was told to go home, back to the Crow's Nest, which he did.

When the owners' grandchildren were young, there was a lot of ghostly activity in the house. Every time their granddaughter would say "Boo!" the smoke alarm would go off. The television would only show cartoons—on every channel—if the children were in the room. Way to go, ghost boy!

While rearranging the furniture in the primary bedroom, Dolly moved a chair away from the wall. Later that night, two men in military uniforms walked through the room.

One took two steps into the room, looked at the bed and then walked away. The other walked in and continued without stopped to look at anything. Dolly feels she may have opened a temporary portal. The grounds on which the Crow's Nest was built may have contained a cemetery at one time. Its graves are said to have been moved to allow for development on the land.

The spirits at the Crow's Nest are so gentle the family dog isn't even bothered by them. He wags his tail vigorously while staring into space—or at a ghost. Unless the dog learns to talk, we will never know for sure, but whatever he sees, he likes it.

Spirits of Lincoln

Lincoln, New Mexico (originally called La Placitas del Rio Bonito), was a one-street town, but it was called "the most dangerous street in America" by President Rutherford B. Hayes. Gunfights were common, and it was a favorite place of Billy the Kid. Many murders occurred along the short stretch of road.

Today, Lincoln is often described as "history frozen in time." The sleepy street of Lincoln is lined with buildings that look much as they would have in 1870, especially the Torreon, a round adobe structure in the middle of town once used for defense. Today, the town celebrates its past with reenactments of famous gunfights and a pageant celebrating its favorite boy bandit, Billy the Kid. Those who come to town are welcome to stay at the Dolan House. That is, if they don't mind sharing their space with a ghost.

This small adobe home was built in 1883 and belonged to James (Jimmy) Dolan and his family. Jimmy Dolan was known to have

a bad temper. People said he was involved in several killings and attempted killings during his years in Lincoln. He was also known for his bad business practices, which included selling illegal beef and price gouging (overcharging).

His bad reputation did not stop Dolan from serving as the treasurer for Lincoln County or serving in the territorial senate. He died at his ranch on February 6, 1898, at the age of forty-nine. His death is widely rumored to have been caused by alcoholism.

But that wasn't the only tragedy the family experienced. Jimmy and his first wife, Caroline,

had four children. Born in 1880, Emil Dolan died at the age of two from disease. Their second daughter, Louise Mabel, died in 1883 shortly after construction of the Dolan House was complete. Caroline died in 1886 during the birth of her last child, Bessie.

It is said the presence of Caroline can still be felt in the room that served as her bedroom, which is the rental suite of the bed-and-breakfast. Perhaps her sadness is what keeps her there, still mourning the children she lost.

The Dolan House isn't the only haunted hotel in town. Since its opening in 1874, the Wortley Hotel has hosted lawmen and outlaws alike, and it saw its fair share of shoot-outs. The place has been through several owners and name changes. It even burned down a couple times!

You can expect to enjoy fine meals during your stay at the Wortley, but the original menu has not been preserved—and everyone should be thankful, because it included Gila monsters (poisonous lizards), rattlesnakes, and bears. Oh, my!

If you visit today, you're likely be greeted by a flock of free-range chickens who are jokingly called the "Wortley Welcoming Committee." A small farm on the property houses goats, pigs, and sheep. Natural wildlife visits regularly as well, so it's not uncommon to see deer and elk on the front lawn. It's hard to imagine this tranquil setting was the location of so much past violence. The owners are quick to point out that no guests have been gunned down in 135 years. But you may encounter some of those unfortunate guests of the past.

The Wortley experiences the usual ghost clues, such as disembodied voices and cold spots. But it is also home

to apparitions that are clearly visible. Guests have reported seeing men in long black coats floating along the hallway or inside their rooms.

During the five-day battle of the Lincoln County War, the hotel was used as a military headquarters. Today, ghost soldiers are sometimes seen crossing the grounds, and ghostly horses can be heard as they travel up the Rio Bonito toward Fort Stanton.

If you like the thought of ghosts that you can see, your chances of spotting one at the Wortley seem pretty strong. The ghosts there aren't confined to one room or area of the hotel. They're everywhere, inside and out.

Chilling Chama

The history of the Chama Valley dates back over a thousand years. The Anasazi people carved and lived in the Puye Cliff Dwellings. The Tewa people built adobes nearby and lived in them until they were abandoned in 1580. When the Spanish arrived, they settled a farm town here, naming it San Joaquin del Rio de Chama. New people began to move to the area once the railroad came though. The post office opened in 1880 under the name of Chama. In its early days, Chama had a reputation as a place with many saloons, a gambling house, and several moonshine stills. This attracted outlaws, but when the boom left Chama, so did most of its rowdier residents.

Chama today is largely a tourist community with the motto "All Roads Lead to Chama." Some people who come never leave. Let's learn about them.

You might meet some of Chama's permanent residents at Foster's Hotel & Restaurant, the oldest commercial structure in Chama, built in 1880. Although Chama suffered a series of devastating fires over the years, Foster's has been spared. The owners think of their hotel as a living piece of history. Constructed of adobe and railroad ties, Foster's is a distinctive landmark. Ghosts seem to have no problem at all finding it.

Guests report hearing a woman coughing and gasping in the hallway. It's believed that those who hear it are listening to the final sounds of a newly elected female judge who was poisoned at the hotel in the 1880s. Allegedly, the men of the town poisoned her because they did not approve of a woman as a judge.

Cries of a young girl are heard in one of the guest rooms at Foster's. She reportedly died from an illness over a hundred years ago, and her distress continues to upset staff and guests. Some have heard her rattling doorknobs. No one knows if she's looking for someone or just being a curious kid.

Distinctive sounds of a cowboy's jangling spurs as he paces the second-floor hallway have sent many curious guests to the front desk looking for answers. A dark shadow reported in Room 21 may be the same spirit. Guests have also noticed cold and hot spots in Room 25. The cowboy ghost might like to switch things up and pace around in a different room now and then.

Service staff report a bothersome ghost who likes to mess up beds and throw pillows on the floor after the beds have been made.

Maybe they're tired of new people constantly sleeping in their bed. Or maybe they think the staff aren't doing a good enough job and they need to try again. You can never be sure with some ghosts.

Haunted Hatch and Rodey

Early Spanish explorers settled in the Hatch Valley in the late 1500s to early 1600s. They established Rodey, the oldest village in the area, and Hatch, as an agricultural sector of New Mexico. The Hatch/Rodey area relied on the backbreaking efforts of farm workers. They grew onions, corn, cotton, alfalfa, lettuce, cabbage, oats, pecans, and chiles such as the now world-famous Hatch chile.

In its earliest days, Rodey was surrounded by walls for protection. Violence was always a possibility back then. There were also floods to contend with. Early settlers had many challenges here. Is that why some of them found it difficult to leave, even after death?

One of the most haunted places in the area is St. Francis de Sales Church. Construction began on the church in 1860. But it took twenty-five years to complete—flooding from the Rio Grande in 1870 stopped the project and forced the whole community to move farther west. Now the church functions as a retreat and event center, but traces of its past can still be found.

Bullets were found encased in the adobe walls when the church was restored. These were believed to be from Old West gunfights that started at a saloon across the street and ended up in the church courtyard. Local legend states residents still hear the gunfights playing out on clear summer evenings.

Given the age of the church, it is not surprising to hear there are ghosts present. There are four known burials on the property, three of which are nearly 150 years old.

Two young priests, possibly brothers, are laid to rest under the floor to the left of the altar. This practice was common at the time. According to church records, one of the young men was murdered and the other died from a severe illness.

Images of shadows have been captured and odd happenings occur within the church, including flickering lights, rushes of cold air, and slamming doors. Some think the priests who are buried under the floor are responsible.

The ashes of a local resident were scattered in the churchyard at his request. His spirit is thought to spend time gently rocking in a chair on the front porch of the casita.

A fifteen-year-old boy, thought to be named Elias, was accidentally shot near here in the late 1880s. It is believed his brother may have been the shooter. His family did not live in the area. They were only passing through, so they brought his body to the church and asked permission to bury him on the grounds. Their request was granted, and the grave of young Elias is below a window of the church in the courtyard behind the bell tower.

Elias's spirit is mischievous and is reported to peer into windows or cause doors to slam and items to move around. His pranks are harmless, but they can be startling.

A figure of a man dressed in priest's robes walks through the casita on his way to the church. He doesn't bother anyone, he just peacefully goes on his way.

Conclusion

I hoped you've enjoyed learning a little more about New Mexico and the ghosts who haunt its beautiful historic hotels and getaways. The state had rough beginnings, but it's a fun and interesting destination now with varied landscapes and activities. It would take a long time to see and experience all that the Land of Enchantment has to offer—perhaps more than a lifetime, based on the number of spirits who have chosen to spend their afterlife there as well.

Shelli Timmons writes for kids of all ages. After many years working with numbers, she realized she liked letters a whole lot more, so she stepped away from the world of finance and entered the realm of stories. She loves old houses and buildings, and is always open to sharing space with a ghost or two. She currently lives in Central Texas in a house much newer than she'd prefer, with an equal number of people and dogs.

Check out some of the other Spooky America titles available now!

Spooky America was adapted from the creeptastic Haunted America series for adults. Haunted America explores historical haunts in cities and regions across America. Each book chronicles both the widely known and less-familiar history behind local ghosts and other unexplained mysteries. Here's more from *Haunted Hotels and Ghostly Getaways of New Mexico* author Donna Blake Birchell:

www.ingramcontent.com/pod-product-compliance
Lightning Source LLC
Chambersburg PA
CBHW070336100426
42812CB00005B/1350